MY EXPERIENCE WITH DEATH

My Experience with Death

ATIYA C. HENLEY

Superior Publishing LLC.

Contents

Dedication	vii
DEATH	1
How Do You Feel About Death?	2
My First Experience With Death	3
Do You Remember Your First Death Experience?	4
GrandMa Ceaster	5
SAM	7
Free Write	11
STORMY	12
Free Write	14

MY COUSIN EICHA	15
Free Write	17
A Sad Time	18
ONE DAY	20
A Happy Time...	21
I Didn't Get To Say It When You Were Here...	23
Weekly Thoughts	25
Weekly Thoughts	28
Weekly Thoughts	31
Weekly Thoughts	34
Weekly Thoughts	37
Weekly Thoughts	40
Weekly Thoughts	43

I want to dedicate this book to my cousin Eicha.
I want to dedicate this book to Aunt Esther Gibson and my Grandma Faye Calvert.
Also to Maree, Nailah and Bray
I love you guys so glad that you are in my life.

Copyright © 2022 by Atiya Henley

All rights reserved. No part of this book may be reproduced in any manner whatsoever without written permission except in the case of brief quotations embodied in critical articles and reviews.

Superior Publishing LLC, 2022

Superior Publishing LLC.
Cedar Bluff, MS
(662) 295-9893

DEATH

My definition of death is when someone or something leaves and you know they will never come back.

I am eleven years old and I had not really experienced death until my cousin Eicha died. I do know that the death of someone you love is not a good feeling. It hurts so bad in your chest. It makes you feel like you can't breathe. This is one of the worst feelings I have ever experienced. The people older than me always tell me that we all have to die. And that when people die if they are saved they are in a better place. Even though that might be true, it does not stop the hurting.

My mom told me that if I wrote about how I felt it would help me and maybe help someone else. So here goes.

How Do You Feel About Death?

My First Experience With Death

My first experience, I can remember going far away to a funeral. I remember it being really cold and I remember seeing snow.

I remember walking in with my family and sitting down. Most of the people I saw, I didn't know. I was very young so I don't remember a whole lot, but I remember when it was time to look into the casket, someone picked me up to look inside. I didn't remember the person inside but I remember she was beautiful. She looked as if she was just sleeping. And that's really all that I remember. `

Do You Remember Your First Death Experience?

GrandMa Ceaster

My mom and I adopted this lady as our Grandma, because it seemed like she didn't have any family. Her name was Ceaster, she was so sweet and soft. I thought she was very funny. We called her Grandma Ceaster. We would always stop by to see her and sit on the porch with her and talk about old times.

One day we stopped and the neighbor's dog was there, she was always there. She was there so much we thought that she was Grandma Ceaster's dog. I was about 4, I guess, and I remember that day when we stopped by and sat on the porch with Grandma that little puppy bit my finger. I snatched my hand and screamed. And my Grandma Ceaster got so mad, she fussed at that little puppy and whipped her. We had never seen her upset like that, she was afraid that the dog had hurt me.

I remember when we found out that she had died it hurt. Even now, every time we pass her house my heart sinks. I really miss her. Sometimes I look out there and just wish that I could hug her again.

SAM

So Sam was my first dog. I did not really know him like that because he was already here before I was even born. He was always tied up. I never could understand why he was always on a chain. But I remember one time he was off the chain and we were both happy. He was so happy, he let me rub him. He licked my hand and my dad was yelling at the other dogs telling them to be quiet but it scared Sam, so he ran off but he came back later.

My mom told me that when she first brought me home from the hospital, he loved me. She said that he was trying to look in the baby carriage to see me. She said that he was smelling the air and whining. She said she would run him off but he kept coming back, sniffing the air and whining. As I got older, he just began to protect me, running off the other dogs and when we would pull up at home, he would run in circles around the entire yard barking until we made it in the house.

I realized at the end of the summer why they kept him on the chain. One morning when the bus came to pick me up for school, Sam tried to get on the bus and get the bus driver. The bus driver was yelling and my parents were yelling.

I couldn't get on the bus because every time the bus driver opened the door he was trying to get on barking loud and vicious. My mom and daddy tried to trick him to get him away from the bus door,so as he ran back toward them, I got on the bus. When Sam realized what had happened he was so mad he chased my bus. After this he was back on the chain until the next summer.

Sam started looking old. He was getting gray around his mouth and then he was acted like he didn't see as well any more. He stopped chasing the cars when he was off the chain. He didn't even try to get on my bus any more. He started sleeping all the time. He had stopped running around the yard barking when we made it home like he used to. Sam had also started staying behind the house where his doghouse was and he wasn't even chained up. When he was asleep he snored so loud. And some days he didn't try to come to the front of the house.

My daddy started saying that he was going to get me a dog to grow up with me, like Sam had grew up with my brother. He wanted another German Shepherd. His brother ended up giving him a white German Shepherd named Snow. And Snow became my dog. We had Snow for about a month. And sometimes during that month, Sam had died. My dad didn't tell me. I found out later. He didn't want me to be sad. So I'm not sure when it happened. My daddy didn't even tell my brother. And when my brother found out it was a few months later. He couldn't believe it. Sam had been in his life since he was seven years old. So they grew up together.

Finding out about Sam hurt. He was a family member. He was a protector. And then he left. He was about seventeen years old. I wonder if dogs really go to a dog heaven?

Free Write

STORMY

She was my grandparent's dog. And she was always very happy to see me.

But she still had a child's mind or maybe I should say a puppy's mind, even though she was grown. She was born before me like Sam was. When Stormy was off the chain she would play with me. I would play under the trees like I was cooking and she would be right there with me. We played like she was another person.

Now this is the hard part to talk about, she was very pretty, but when she started to grow old, she started getting bags under her eyes and she started to stink. And when she walked sometimes she would fall. Her hair was sticking to her was kind of weird. I knew she was getting old like Sam. But one night, I was lying on my grandmother and she showed me a picture and I was like, "Awww" she was very pretty as a puppy. I told my grandmother that she needed to take a picture of her now even though she didn't look so good. Then she told me that she couldn't because she's up there with God and I was confused. I was looking at her like she was confused. I was about to say she is at her dog pin but she told me to read her post on Facebook. So I read it and it said that Stormy had died. I was hollering and crying like a baby and it seemed like anytime someone said her name I got emotional.

It seemed like death was taking all of our dogs.

Free Write

MY COUSIN EICHA

When I found out my cousin Eicha had died, I cried so hard! I was hoping that it was just a joke, but it wasn't, it was real. Sometimes I find myself saying it's a prank and it's not real. I wasn't expecting her to die, it was so unexpected, that's why I still don't believe that it's true. When I found out I just fell to the ground, it felt like my legs couldn't take it and I couldn't stop crying. I was just pouring out. My heart was feeling bad. I was wishing that I could do something but God had the final word. I just wanted her to stay here. I couldn't eat. I couldn't do anything. I don't know if she was in pain or not on earth but I knew that she had to be in heaven because she was an angel.

Eicha was so pretty and she had some pretty glowing skin. I never heard anyone say anything bad about her because she was very sweet. She had a beautiful smile and she always showed it. She was my cousin, but I looked up to her like an Aunt.

When I first met her it was at my Grandma Faye house. She was here and I walked down to my Aunt Esther's house and that's when I found out who she was. She spent time with her nieces and nephews and me. I remember when she took us to the Candy Lady's house and a dog tried to get to us. She grabbed a stick and stood there to protect us. She was a real soldier because she got us back safely.

She was one of my daddy's favorite cousins. I knew that she loved me because she really loved my daddy. I hate that she's gone but I know that we will see each other again someday.

Free Write

A Sad Time

ONE DAY

One day, I will meet God and all of the people that I have written about. There will be no more worries. I will get to meet all those that I have heard about and didn't know, like my great grandparents that I have heard so many stories about. One day I believe I will meet them in Heaven with My Lord.

A Happy Time...

I didn't get to say it
when you were here...

Dear

Weekly Thoughts

Monday Thoughts:

Tuesday Thoughts:

Wednesday Thoughts:

Thursday Thoughts:

Friday Thoughts:

Saturday Thoughts:

Sunday Thoughts:

Weekly Thoughts

Monday Thoughts:

Tuesday Thoughts:

Wednesday Thoughts:

Thursday Thoughts:

Friday Thoughts:

Saturday Thoughts:

Sunday Thoughts:

Weekly Thoughts

Monday Thoughts:

Tuesday Thoughts:

Wednesday Thoughts:

Thursday Thoughts:

Friday Thoughts:

Saturday Thoughts:

Sunday Thoughts:

Weekly Thoughts

Monday Thoughts:

Tuesday Thoughts:

Wednesday Thoughts:

Thursday Thoughts:

Friday Thoughts:

Saturday Thoughts:

Sunday Thoughts:

Weekly Thoughts

Monday Thoughts:

Tuesday Thoughts:

Wednesday Thoughts:

Thursday Thoughts:

Friday Thoughts:

Saturday Thoughts:

Sunday Thoughts:

Weekly Thoughts

Monday Thoughts:

Tuesday Thoughts:

Wednesday Thoughts:

Thursday Thoughts:

Friday Thoughts:

Saturday Thoughts:

Sunday Thoughts:

Weekly Thoughts

Monday Thoughts:

Tuesday Thoughts:

Wednesday Thoughts:

Thursday Thoughts:

Friday Thoughts:

Saturday Thoughts:

Sunday Thoughts:

www.ingramcontent.com/pod-product-compliance
Lightning Source LLC
Chambersburg PA
CBHW052126110526
44592CB00013B/1771